THE KICK-ASS
INSIDER'S GUIDE TO
KETTLEBELL COMPLEXES

ALEKS SALKIN

This publication is Copyright © 2025 Aleks Salkin (the "Author"). All Rights Reserved. Published in the United States of America. The legal notices, disclosures, and disclaimers within this publication are copyrighted by the Law Office of Michael E. Young PLLC and licensed for use by the Author and Publisher in this publication. All rights reserved.

No part of this publication may be reproduced or transmitted in any form or by any means, electronic or mechanical, including photocopying, recording, or by an information storage and retrieval system -- except by a reviewer who may quote brief passages in a review to be printed in a magazine, newspaper, blog, or website -- without permission in writing from the Author. For information, please contact the Author by e-mail at aleks@alekssalkin.com.

For more information, please read the "Disclosures and Disclaimers" section at the end of this publication.

First Print Edition, January 2025

Published by Salkin Strength Solutions LLC (the "Publisher").

TABLE OF CONTENTS

Acknowledgements 5
Foreword by Dan John 7
Stop Right There! 11
In The Beginning… 15
"What The Heck is a Complex?" 19
"Who the hell are you? And why should I listen to you?" 24
Real World Complexes, Real World Strength 28
Soviet Weightlifters Discover (Then Get Sucker Punched With) Barbell Complexes 35
Why Kettlebells ROCK For Complex Training 39
The Hidden Benefits of Complexes 41
Putting Together an Effective Complex 47
- ◦ #1: The Aim of the Complex 47
- ◦ #2: Number of Kettlebells 49
- ◦ #3: The Flow, or The "Anti-Flow" 51

The Programming 56
The Complexes 59
- ◦ Strength Complex Day 59
- ◦ Hypertrophy Complex Day 60
- ◦ Endurance Complex Day 61

Rules of Engagement 63
Movement: The Missing Link and '5th Element' of
Real-World Strength 66
- The Original Strength RESETS 67
- Stretching and Mobility 71
- Chair Twists 73
- Hanging 74
- Quad Stretches 75
- Hamstring Stretches 77
- Eagle's Eye View 78

Before You Begin... 81
Train and Gain with Aleks 97
All Gain, NO Pain! 101
Disclosures and Disclaimers 123

ACKNOWLEDGEMENTS

"No man is an island."

English Poet John Donne

As much as I'd love to claim sole and exclusive credit for the success of this book, as with anything, it was an endeavor that was made infinitely better through the help of others.

First, the great and wise Dan John, who was kind enough to give the book a read through and gladly give it a most excellent foreword.

Second, my friend and bona fide kettlebell master Geoff Neupert – aka "Captain Complex" – for reading the book early on and offering his helpful and insightful suggestions on how to make the book better and more impactful to readers.

Third, my coach, mentor, and friend Scott Stevens of Omaha Elite Kettlebell for not only teaching me the kettlebell kung fu all those years ago (16 years, as of the publishing of this book), but for teaming up to help me with the videos for the free *Kick-Ass Insider's Guide to Kettlebell Complexes* Video Resource Center.

And finally, YOU, the reader, for investing in this book and being willing to put the principles, precepts, practices, and programming contained within to the ultimate test: **your own training.**

I am sincerely grateful.

FOREWORD BY DAN JOHN

The modern kettlebell movement began around the start of the millennium. Certainly, and you will often find this argued endlessly in the crazier forums on the internet, the KB has been around a long time. My first exposure was in 1974 (or so...memory is a funny thing) when I watched the Soviet hammer throwers destroy a perfectly fine lawn with a variety of throwing drills. When asked about this equipment, the Russians used the word "pood" and, as things often happen in history, the word "pud" became synonymous with overweight track and field throwing drills.

When John Ducane and Pavel sat down at a coffee shop and discussed making and marketing the KBs, I'm not sure anyone realized a quarter century or so later that we would see pharmaceutical ads on television with people moving kettlebells. One can find horrible brands of KBs sold at most chain stores...and, trust me, you get what you pay for here.

If I were to sum the biggest issues still with KBs after all this time is the total misunderstanding of what the tool (the KB) should be used for by most of us. Powerlifters lose their minds discussing KBs because the loads are too light, and the exercises don't reflect their training. Bodybuilders instantly tried to figure out how to pump their biceps and disliked the thickness of the grip. Wrong tool for the wrong job.

ALEKS "THE HEBREW HAMMER" SALKIN

Kettlebells, first and foremost, teach movement. From there, the KB shows us how to build strength using time (time under tension) as an instructor and conditioning by using time (when will this end?) as a taskmaster. All of this comes together with complexes.

Aleks Salkin's work on KB complexes, The Kick-Ass Insider's Guide to Kettlebell Complexes, blends the best of the historic tradition of strength training with the truly marvelous insights of the past quarter-century. There is a depth to this book that allows the reader to sit back and see the long tradition of complexes (and circuit training) that is part of the story of all strength and conditioning. Then, Aleks puts together some brilliantly simple approaches to the complexity of complexes.

All too often, modern personal trainers, coaches, and fitness experts seem clueless on the concepts of complexes and their close cousin, circuit training. I use complexes daily in my training and the athletes I work with in any and all sports. As you will find in this book, there is a history, a tradition, of using the barbell, dumbbell and kettlebell with back to back to back exercises.

I grew up on barbells and I still love lifting and training with the Olympic lifts and the whole family of barbell strength exercises. I do use barbell complexes, but Aleks has convinced me that the true "king" of complexes is the kettlebell. What really got me thinking is Aleks's discussion of "flow" versus "anti-flow" complex arrangements. With the barbell, transitioning from back squats to, for example, rows, takes a lot of maneuvering for the athlete. With KBs, you basically have the rack and the overhead lockout to think about and the complexes can be, well, "anti-flow" for conditioning.

In performance, we focus on performance...and that makes sense. Aleks points out that different complexes with the kettlebell can

THE KICK-ASS INSIDER'S GUIDE TO KETTLEBELL COMPLEXES

achieve a variety of goals. We have strength, hypertrophy, and conditioning complexes outlined and explained in this book as well a wealth of simply reasonable, doable, and repeatable training programs and ideas.

Don't miss the last section, he also paraphrases Ron Swanson here which is always fun, where Aleks notes the importance of Tim Anderson's Original Strength as well as some basic flexibility work. This is where I think the text shines the most: long-term success in training relies on much more than "Six Days to Six-Pack Abs." This is a training system for everyone and the programs work.

If you want to amp up your training in the quiet confines of a small apartment or beside a lake, this is the training plan for you. If you want to take on a challenge of whole-body transformation, you have the master plan here for you.

It's that simple: do complexes!

Dan John

www.DanJohnUniversity.com
Master kettlebell instructor
All-American discus thrower
Olympic Weightlifting and Highland Games competitor
American Record Holder in the Weight Pentathalon
Creator of the World-Famous Armor Building Complex

ALEKS "THE HEBREW HAMMER" SALKIN

Dan John (right) and the author enjoying breakfast and trading training insights in Omaha, NE

STOP RIGHT THERE!

Read This First...

You are about to embark on a kick-ass journey to what many would say is the ULTIMATE approach to using kettlebells to build brute strength, explosive power, never-say-die conditioning, and unyielding mental toughness *all at the same time*.

Wouldn't it be nice to make sure you're getting the MOST out of your workouts?

I sure think so.

It's one thing to read some pithy words on the printed page – it's another thing entirely to SEE the movements and complexes you're about to be doing in action.

ALEKS "THE HEBREW HAMMER" SALKIN

With that in mind, I put together the FREE **Kick-Ass Insider's Guide to Kettlebell Complexes** Video Resource Center to help guide you on your noble path to glorious gains.

In these free videos I'll show you:

Common kettlebell technique mistakes you might be making *without even realizing it* – and how to eliminate them (sometimes in as little as a few seconds!)

Detailed video demonstrations of each of the complexes featured in this book – including some sneaky HIDDEN strategies and tactics to help you conquer fatigue as it builds up, so you can still triumphantly dominate each and every workout!

Some of my favorite "insider tactics" to set you up for stronger, more effective kettlebell lifting – BEFORE you even begin your first rep!

PLUS, an extra BONUS surprise for you.

It's like having a personal trainer in the palm of your hand!

All you have to do is go to the link below, enter your name and best email address, and I'll whisk you away to the Land of Epic Gains:

www.KettlebellComplex.com

Or, you can point your phone's camera at the QR code below, click the link that pops up, and be guided directly to the page to join the free Video Resource Center.

THE KICK-ASS INSIDER'S GUIDE TO KETTLEBELL COMPLEXES

Point your smartphone's camera at that funny-looking box in the circle above and an option to open up a link will pop up on your screen. Click it and you'll be whisked away to the page to join the FREE Video Resource Center.

Oh, and one more thing...

If you're REALLY eager to hop into the fast lane to fast *gains* in your quest to positively transform your body inside and out – crafting shapely, head-turning amounts of muscle, chiseling eye-popping, jealousy-inducing strength, and re-invigorating yourself with new and exciting levels of unbridled physical and mental confidence you haven't had since your youth (or maybe EVER), one of the best ways to do that is by working with me 1-on-1 so I can help you jump your progress into hyperspace – like Han Solo commandeering the Millenium Falcon (and yes, that means improving your performance even if you feel your own Soft Machine is nought but a rickety "bucket of bolts" like that old smuggler's legendary space ship).

ALEKS "THE HEBREW HAMMER" SALKIN

Details on how to do that can be found at the end of this book.

Without further ado, let's get this journey started...

IN THE BEGINNING...

Since the dawn of recorded history, mankind has sought to get STRONGER.

In ancient Egyptian tombs there are murals depicting men and women exercising with weighted implements such as weighted bags and stones.

"One more rep, bro, it's all you!"

India pioneered training with clubs of various sizes for the training of their wrestlers and warriors.

ALEKS "THE HEBREW HAMMER" SALKIN

India's Berserker-in-Chief 'The Great Gama'

The ancient Greeks were known to lift heavy stones, dumbbells called *halteres*, and perform calisthenics (in fact, the very word *calisthenics* itself comes from two Greek words *kalos sthenos* – "beautiful strength").

THE KICK-ASS INSIDER'S GUIDE TO KETTLEBELL COMPLEXES

Keep in mind this isn't just some idealized physique; some ancient Greek dude actually had to pose for this statue. An impressive physique in every way but one.

Heck, so devoted were the old school Greeks to strength and physical culture there is even a legend about the wrestler Milo that said he carried a calf on his shoulder every single day for years until it was a full-grown bull!

ALEKS "THE HEBREW HAMMER" SALKIN

While the implements may have evolved from bags of sand, stones, and unwitting farm animals into dumbbells, barbells, and kettlebells, one thing has stayed the same: **our desire to conquer our surroundings and get stronger along the way.**

And while the implements themselves are certainly important – given that each of the major ones has its own set of benefits – as time has gone on both science and experience have given rise to a variety of innovative and ruthlessly effective ways of increasing our strength with less guesswork, less wailing and gnashing of teeth, and more predictable and repeatable results.

One such technique that has seen a meteoric rise in popularity over the last few decades has been **complexes**.

"WHAT THE HECK IS A COMPLEX?"

When most of us think of the word "complex", we think of more of "complicated" – a situation wherein something is dizzyingly multi-faceted, confusing, and what have you.

And when it comes to kettlebell and bodyweight training, about the last thing most people want is "complicated" training.

So it may be somewhat ironic that in the world of kettlebells, one of the fastest, finest, and most phenomenal ways of getting leaner, stronger, more skilled, better conditioned, and tougher all around is through a method known as...**complexes!**

And believe it or not, the term "complex" is an apt one – particularly given the fact that the actual definition closely resembles what an eagle's eye view of a kettlebell complex would automatically reveal:

---

complex
[complex] 🔊

ADJECTIVE

1. consisting of many different and connected parts.
   "a complex network of water channels"
   synonyms: compound · composite · compounded · multiplex

So what *is* a "kettlebell complex" exactly?

As Geoff Neupert, retired Master SFG, defines it in his classic book *Kettlebell Muscle*, a complex is:

> *"...a series of exercises performed in a sequence with the same weight and without rest. All the reps for a given exercise are performed first, before moving on to the next exercise."*

Not to be confused with another very popular method of training multiple exercises in succession, a circuit, which is defined in John Little's *Bruce Lee: The Art of Expressing the Human Body* as:

> *"...one complete performance of a group of movements (usually five or six different exercises), each of which targets a different body part. The underlying idea of such training is never to exercise the same muscle group twice in succession, but rather to move on – immediately – to another muscle or body part."*

The latter approach to training – *circuits* – was popularized by a gent named Bob Gajda (GUY-duh), who created a system he called PHA, or *Peripheral Heart Action*, which sought to circulate the blood throughout the body rather than letting it "congest" in just one spot.

THE KICK-ASS INSIDER'S GUIDE TO KETTLEBELL COMPLEXES

Bob Gajda. Looks like he may have known a thing or two.

Sounds a little hocus pocus-y, but it was super popular back in the '60s; so much so that even the great Bruce Lee took to adopting this as one of his preferred methods of training. And while this is pure speculation on my part, I'm sure that the popularity of this and similar systems led to the rise in popularity of exercise machines such as the Marcy Circuit Trainer (which Bruce Lee was also a fan of and owned two of – one he kept in California, the other in Hong Kong) and other big, space-sucking exercise machines.

ALEKS "THE HEBREW HAMMER" SALKIN

In any case, before I go on too much longer of a tangent, here's the takeaway:

Bruce Lee – always ahead of his time – rightly recognized the benefits of doing multiple exercises back-to-back to better train for his activity of choice: kickin' ass.

He figured that if he could keep his blood circulation at high levels all throughout his workouts, he would get some major benefits in his muscular strength, endurance, and even flexibility.

If only the Little Dragon had had Pavel's hardstyle kettlebell approach at his fingertips back in the 60s, he might have just blown away even his own expectations and replaced his big, bulky circuit trainer machine with a sleek and easy-to-store set of kettlebells for all of his strength, endurance, and flexibility needs.

While we can always ponder and theorize about those things, it's important to note that complexes – which, again, offer NO rest between exercises – didn't originate with Pavel Tsatsouline, the King of Kettlebells and primary driver behind the triumphant return of the kettlebell into the Western consciousness at the dawn of the 21st century.

In fact, complexes didn't originate with kettlebells or even with weight training as we know it today!

I would argue that complexes originated with none other than **the very act of lifting itself.**

Complexes are arguably the most NATURAL form of lifting, where the goal is not to compete or to exercise or lift for the sake of lifting, but rather to manipulate the world around us in order to successfully perform a task using strength as a primary physical skill to accomplish it.

THE KICK-ASS INSIDER'S GUIDE TO KETTLEBELL COMPLEXES

Think about professions whose practitioners have a reputation of being strong as a result of their work.

In probably NONE of them are their tasks ever *"pick this heavy thing up and then put it down. Do that several times in a row and then take a long rest."* Whatever lifting or physical labor they're doing has to actually accomplish something, and leaving the weight or object in the same place where it started is – in most cases – not actually all that useful.

(Don't misunderstand: there's nothing wrong with this approach for getting strong in general, as it can still make you very strong. It's just not a scenario we find often outside of standardized exercise.)

Instead, their tasks typically call for them to do several things in a row with a heavy object in order to make it useful for their task at hand.

But before we go on, there's probably already at least one question burning a hole in your mind, aching for an answer…

"WHO THE HELL ARE YOU? AND WHY SHOULD I LISTEN TO YOU?"

Howdy. My name is Aleks Salkin. Or as my friends, fans, and followers in the fitness world call me, *The Hebrew Hammer*

Not just a clever nickname.

A little about me:

I was born and raised in Omaha, Nebraska to a mother who was a competitive gymnast as a youngster and a father who owned a car body shop for many years and learned Karate in his spare time. And while you'd think that would've given me a running head start for a life of raw physicality and confident athletic abilities, you'd be sorely mistaken. In reality those skills must've skipped a generation, because I was scrawny, weak, and almost comically uncoordinated.

In fact, some of my athletic "achievements" as a youth included:

- Being picked 2nd to last in just about every team sport in elementary and middle school
- Getting pinned on a bench press whose weight was roughly that of a broomstick with two bagels on it while in high school
- Being asked "So, is it, like, hard for you to open doors?" by a wise-cracking friend of mine while we lifted weights in a mutual friend's basement in college

Yet despite all that, I knew I wasn't a lost cause. There just HAD to be some way for me to get stronger, fitter, and more physically confident that I just hadn't discovered yet. For all my physical flaws, one thing I got right is that I REFUSED to give up.

Then one day in early 2008 I got a call from a friend of mine asking if I wanted to come over and try a "kettlebell workout". Being young, curious, and forever in search of adventure, I said yes.

And while I don't remember much of the details of the workout, what I do remember is how it made me feel: STRONG. In fact, the kettlebell and the movements I learned to do with it simply felt like an extension of my body: natural, authentic, and POWERFUL.

From that day forward I was hooked.

I made it my mission to learn as much about kettlebell training – and later calisthenics and human movement as well – from the best of the best around the world.

Founder of the modern kettlebell movement Pavel Tsatsouline (left), world-renowned strength coach Dan John (right), Yours Jewly (middle) at Pavel's kettlebell certification in Orlando, FL in 2010

I've since gone on to teach live, in-person workshops and seminars to countless people in 6 different countries (United States, Israel, Italy, Australia, Czech Republic, and Slovakia) with more to come in the very near future.

And my popular daily email tips and online training resources have attracted readers and devotees from even MORE countries, all seeking to conquer the frustration, disappointment, and lackluster

THE KICK-ASS INSIDER'S GUIDE TO KETTLEBELL COMPLEXES

results they've gotten from more conventional methods of kettlebell, calisthenics, and movement training.

And unlike most of my colleagues in the fitness sphere, because I didn't start out as some stud or natural athlete, but rather as a completely awkward and uncoordinated nerd, I had to learn the REAL process for getting stronger, more powerful, and more muscular, rather than the approaches taught by the various life-long athletes who join the fitness industry – disconnected as they are with how real people need to be taught – so my "Hammer Heads" (my affectionate name for my followers) can avoid the all-too-common pipeline of a few weeks of hopeful and exciting gains, followed by months and sometimes even YEARS of painful setbacks, physical maladies, and a sense of hopelessness.

I'll tell you more about how that works at the end of this book.

For now, let's get back to the topic at hand:

How complexes help you build real-world strength.

REAL WORLD COMPLEXES, REAL WORLD STRENGTH

Farmers

Farm work contains too many examples to list them all out, but let's take a look at the ubiquitous baling hay – or moving large bales of hay from one area to another.

Here's what that complex looks like:

- Lift the hay bale and prop it against the legs

THE KICK-ASS INSIDER'S GUIDE TO KETTLEBELL COMPLEXES

- Walk the hay bale to the area where it will be stacked
- Heave the bale up to chest level
- Throw it onto a trailer

Do that for an hour or an entire afternoon and you'll suddenly understand how otherwise skinny farmers can chump you in just about any strength feat. You'll also understand the value of complexes.

Mechanics

Though a lot of the work mechanics do involves more small manipulation of various doohickeys and doodads within a car's engine (I'm very mechanically inclined, as you can tell), working in a machine shop, as my dad used to, often involves a lot more heavy physical activity.

Here's one example of a complex my dad told me he used to have to do while working on cylinder heads in his old body shop:

ALEKS "THE HEBREW HAMMER" SALKIN

- Remove the cylinder head from the shelf
- Set it on the ground
- Lift it off the ground
- Walk it over to a work bench
- Set it on the ground again
- Lift it off the ground again
- Set it on the work bench

And this is only one example of the everyday heavy lifting he used to do.

In fact, the "training" he got in his machine shop was so effective that despite his small stature, he told me that when he started working out at a local gym he was able to easily max out several of the exercise machines while many of the recreational bodybuilders there were often training with only half of what he was lifting!

THE KICK-ASS INSIDER'S GUIDE TO KETTLEBELL COMPLEXES

Firefighters

Firefighters are especially renowned not just for their bravery, but also their incredible strength and fitness levels – a must for their line of work.

One example of a complex that a firefighter must do would include:

- Lifting someone off the floor of a burning house or building
- Carrying them to the ladder
- Carrying them down the ladder
- Carrying them to the ambulance

And this is only one small example. According to my friend Derek McMillin (pictured above), a captain on the Omaha, Nebraska fire department and certified paramedic, firefighting is replete with scenarios that could be considered complexes due to the multiple challenging tasks that need to be done back-to-back:

==

> ...every single time we make a fire [run] of even an automatic fire detection it is a "complex".
>
> You step off the rig wearing an additional 70-90 lbs of gear, then have to traverse landscaping, cut down fences, do forced entry into a building with Halligan bars/sledge hammers or using 60 lb jaws of life to spread doors open. Only then does the work actually start, where you mask up, then crawl to the fire dragging heavy-ass hose lines past corners in homes. They get stuck on doors, around couches, kitchen appliances.
>
> If at that point you do have a viable rescue, you drop what you're doing and... you have to then backpedal out of the home.
>
> It's an incredibly dynamic, physical job. The act of vertical ventilation is absolutely exhausting. You gear up, then have to set an aluminum heavy-ass commercial grade ladder and carry chain saws and axes to the roof. You then go on air and have to cut a 4×4 or larger ventilation hole on the roof.
>
> We have to do this job regardless of weather. Sweltering hot, or -40 degrees through snow drifts and ice.

==

THE KICK-ASS INSIDER'S GUIDE TO KETTLEBELL COMPLEXES

No matter how you cut it, in many of the most essential and important jobs in the world are made possible by complexes.

You!

Yes, that's right, YOU have probably unknowingly done some complexes in your day, too. If you've ever flown on an airplane with carry-on luggage, odds are you have done the following:

- Carry your luggage to your seat
- Curl it to your chest
- Press it into the overhead compartment

You might have even had to toss in a little bonus challenge by rearranging everybody else's stuff so you can get yours in. That's enough of a workout to truly earn that Bloody Mary you're gonna order on board at 10 am on a Thursday.

Although nowadays we are fortunate enough to live in times where hard physical labor purely for our survival is largely a thing of the past, even in the distant past when life was rugged and survival wasn't guaranteed, some ambitious people decided they wanted to continue to test their mettle against the world in general and gravity in particular and started standardizing the jolly old game of taming iron with regimented exercise routines, specially designed weights, and more.

The elements we're now familiar with – sets, reps, rest periods, and so on – became part and parcel of the process, as did the act of doing several exercises back-to-back in complex form, I'm sure.

Though we may never know exactly when and where complexes stepped out of the world of real-life physical labor and into the more sanitized and organized world of exercise, at some point someone decided that the art of lifting should imitate the life of laboring, and so complexes morphed from the realm of physical work into workouts. It may come as no surprise to learn where they were honed, sharpened, and outright *weaponized* as a tactic against weakness and physical inferiority...**The now (thankfully) defunct Soviet Union.**

SOVIET WEIGHTLIFTERS DISCOVER (THEN GET SUCKER PUNCHED WITH) BARBELL COMPLEXES

Many moons ago, my friend and performing strongman "The Iron Tamer" Dave Whitley surmised that kettlebell sport could have only originated in Russia. The reason: life in Russia is so hard that the only way to make it more bearable was to invent a sport like kettlebell sport that sucked so much and was so ungodly difficult that once you were done, everything else felt downright easy and pleasant.

Humor aside, you have to wonder if the same mindset didn't apply to the Soviets' ample use of complexes as well.

Romanian strength and conditioning coach Emeritus, Istvan Javorek, not only popularized the use of complexes in his home country, but also throughout the US, where he defected to in the 1980s.

ALEKS "THE HEBREW HAMMER" SALKIN

Istvan "Steve" Javorek

Revolutionary Olympic lifter and the first man to military press over 500 lbs, Vasily Alexeev, was a big fan of barbell complexes for crushing weakness and forging over-the-top levels of brutal strength all the live-long day.

THE KICK-ASS INSIDER'S GUIDE TO KETTLEBELL COMPLEXES

Vasily Alexeev in his prime

According to an interviewer of Alexeev, Dmitri Ivanov:

> *"Usually the athletes lift barbells and then immediately drop them. This takes several seconds.*
> *According to Alexeev's method, the athlete finds himself under the weight for a period of two or three minutes. The entire body must sustain this prolonged effort, as the athlete completes several consecutive exercises without letting go of the equipment.*
> *The weight of the barbell is relatively light, but the varied work with it affects every muscle cell.*
> *By the end of the two-week session, all of Alexeev's students had increased their bodyweight as a result of muscle growth – and at the same time they'd increased their abilities."*

ALEKS "THE HEBREW HAMMER" SALKIN

In other words, bucking the trend of doing only one exercise at a time (as was the preferred method in those days) and only going heavy, Alexeev didn't give a crap about anything conventional, and preferred to do something "heretical", particularly in the world of Olympic lifting, by string exercises together in a complex.

The result of his endeavors was super strong, muscular, and tough-as-nails students.

And though his approach was originally devised for barbells, and can also be done with dumbbells, the kettlebell is arguably an even BETTER tool for just such an exercise arrangement. Why? For several reasons:

WHY KETTLEBELLS ROCK FOR COMPLEX TRAINING

Apart from just being fun to train with in general, there are some real, practical reasons why kettlebells rock for complex training even above and beyond other great implements like the barbell and dumbbells.

#1: Kettlebells Are More Forgiving

Whether you like barbells or not (and I sure do) they are awkward. With barbells, YOU have to conform your body around the cold, uncaring bar. This is one of the reasons why so many people find the barbell tweaks them more often than not, whereas they can push the limit a bit easier with kettlebells. And by contrast, kettlebells work WITH the natural movements of your body rather than demanding that your body move around it.

#2: Kettlebells Are More Accessible

Connected with the above observation, kettlebells are more accessible to more people as the learning curve is, by and large, much shorter. Even "advanced" kettlebell movements like snatches and jerks can be much more easily achieved with a kettlebell by your Average Joe than a barbell snatch or jerk, which largely favor young, uninjured, and very mobile athletes.

#3: Kettlebells Are (Arguably) Much Safer

Because of the fatigue factor, the fact that kettlebells conform to the movements of the body rather than demanding the reverse like barbells do, as well as their accessibility to exercise enthusiasts rather than competitive strength athletes alone, kettlebells are a no-brainer for complexes.

To put a cherry on top, as Pavel says in his landmark *Return of the Kettlebell*: "Catch many barbell reps of either of these drills (jerk or push press) and you will look and feel like you have lost a UFC fight."

Now, you may be saying to yourself "okay, cool, so you CAN do complexes with kettlebells, and you can do them well...but why SHOULD you?"

"Should", is, of course, a matter of choice – or to be more specific, a matter of your goals.

Without question there are some goals that not only don't require you to do complexes, but are better accomplished WITHOUT them.

There are, however, a variety of unique and highly valuable benefits of complexes that you would be hard-pressed to get using other training methods. Let's look at a few of them.

THE HIDDEN BENEFITS OF COMPLEXES

In addition to my contention just a few short pages ago that complexes are simply one of the most natural forms of lifting, there are plenty of other reasons to do them. For instance:

#1: Complexes can help 'connect' seemingly unrelated kettlebell skills together

Many moons ago I had the pleasure of having dinner with now Master SFG (StrongFirst kettlebell instructor) Jon Engum in Omaha, NE after he conducted a few workshops on kettlebells and flexibility training.

During the dinner, he talked about how strength coach and world-renowned kettlebell expert Dan John had once noted (and I paraphrase):

> "All the kettlebell exercises are kind of like a big extended family. If you look at one individually, and then another one, you may not really see the resemblance. But once you see them all – like in a big family photo – you start to see the similarities that they all have in common."

And what better way is there to "see" multiple exercises back-to-back than by actually *feeling* them back-to-back?

While we have a tendency to see each kettlebell exercise as a completely separate skill, the truth is that each one has a lot in common with the others – including the slow grinds with the fast ballistics.

Doing them back-to-back helps you see and feel what they have in common with one another, which holds a lot of potential for simplifying and speeding up your mastery of the moves.

#2: Complexes can improve your technique (if done properly)

I feel the need to include the caveat of "if done properly" since, of course, a sloppy slapping together of moves will do you no good. Things have to make sense, and this is true of your complexes no matter your level of familiarity with ye olde kettlebell.

And while complexes are typically viewed as a more intermediate or advanced tactic, the truth is that – if programmed intelligently – they can potentially be valuable for the beginner looking to improve his or her technique as well.

For example:

Let's say you're a beginner who has just begun to learn the kettlebell kung fu, and your main aim is to dominate the swing so you can unlock the various other ballistic kettlebell skills that will help you take your strength, stamina, and all-around toughness to new and greater heights. Bully for you.

Well, one of the things I've noticed in my many years of teaching is that a lot of beginners seem to struggle with going from the deadlift to the swing.

Although deadlifts and swings are both based on the same movement pattern – *the hip hinge* – they are very different in

THE KICK-ASS INSIDER'S GUIDE TO KETTLEBELL COMPLEXES

their execution: deadlifts are a grind, and thus by their nature are a slower movement. Swings, on the other hand, are a ballistic movement, and indeed most people's first introduction to ballistic movements at large.

So how do you bridge this gap effectively and efficiently to speed up the learning process WITHOUT putting yourself (or your trainee) at risk of developing shoddy technique or maybe getting tweaked?

One way would be through a simple complex (almost sounds like a contradiction, huh? "Simple complex" – like "true lies").

	Movement	**Reps**
A1	Deadlift	5
A2	Hike*	5
A3	Power Swing**	5
A4	Swing	5

If you look closely, you'll notice that this complex helps you (or your trainee) connect several swing progressions together in one smooth, continuous flow, thereby making it easier to understand the significance of each one of them while (almost) effortlessly building up a greater level of skill and familiarity with the swing.

This approach can work well for just about any kettlebell movement and allows you or your trainee to not only improve the kettlebell skills in question, but also get in a heck of a workout as well.

> *a hike is the part of the swing where you toss the kettlebell back between your legs – much like the hike in an American football game

**power swings are where you return the kettlebell on the ground in front of you in the starting position after each rep. This technique makes it easier for most people to learn both the timing of the swing as well as how to generate the power necessary to make each rep explosive.

#3: Complexes can help "stress test" your technique

As you might imagine, the longer you hold onto something, the more fatiguing it becomes (true for both kettlebell training AND life in general, as it turns out).

And while seeking out fatigue is not exactly the point of kettlebell or calisthenics training, it nevertheless will rear its head and challenge you to a duel – a duel that you can either succumb to or conquer.

Let's use the example from above of the kettlebell swing complex.

Your first round will probably be no sweat. The second one may be a little more challenging, but no big deal. By the third round you might start to notice you can't exactly mentally drift off; you have to be really present and focused to make sure you're not letting bad habits or bad technique creep in.

So if you were to do a total of 5 rounds of deadlift ⇒ hike ⇒ power swing ⇒ swing, with each drill getting 5 reps, you'd have done a mere 20 reps of standard swings, but 80 reps in all, thus challenging you to keep those 20 reps looking strong despite all the other work you've done. And naturally the same holds true with other movements as well.

THE KICK-ASS INSIDER'S GUIDE TO KETTLEBELL COMPLEXES

#4: Complexes allow you to get a lot of quality work done in very little time

Let's face it: unless you're young, unattached, and have no real responsibilities in life, you probably don't have an hour or an hour and a half to workout anymore (but those were the days, weren't they?) If you've got big ambitions and paltry little time to meet them, what you CAN'T afford to fiddle around with is

- Long commutes to and from a gym
- Long, meandering workouts
- Super complicated programming

Instead, what you need is something, short, time-efficient, and ruthlessly effective at smashing weakness, forging brute strength, and making you look more sexually appealing (because let's be honest, whether it's the main effect or side effect of our workouts, everybody wants to look good nekkid).

And what could be more time efficient than waltzing over to your 'Courage Corner' (an old-school term for a workout space), knocking out a few rounds of a kettlebell complex, and calling it a day, knowing that when you take your shirt off at the beach or the local pool during the Summer months you're going to turn heads?

#5: Complexes are highly effective for getting leaner, more muscular, and stronger

Contrary to popular belief, kettlebell complexes are good for more than just metabolic conditioning (although they are truly stellar for that).

As previously mentioned, when talking about the Soviet weightlifters who discovered the power of complexes for themselves and their students, greater levels of lean body mass AND brute strength can both be achieved with complexes in addition to simply getting in better shape as well.

And are these not THE main reason most of us train to begin with?

So now the question remains: *how do we put together an effective complex?*

I'm glad you (theoretically) asked.

From my perspective, there are at least 3 factors to consider:

1. the aim of the complex
2. number of kettlebells
3. the flow, or "anti-flow"

Let's take a look at each factor:

PUTTING TOGETHER AN EFFECTIVE COMPLEX

#1: The Aim of the Complex

"If you don't know where you're going, any road will get you there."

The Mad Hatter, Alice in Wonderland

By now you don't need me or anyone else to tell you just how diverse kettlebell training is. Whether it's strength, muscle-building, or endurance you're after, the mighty kettlebell can do it all.

But the key is that you have to know exactly which of those things you want to achieve!

The reason why is simple: different aims require three different things:

- Rep ranges

ALEKS "THE HEBREW HAMMER" SALKIN

- Number of exercises
- Rest intervals
- Weight of kettlebells

For example, for strength, my recommendation would be:

- Between 2-5 exercises
- Between 1-5 reps per exercise
- 3 minutes rest between rounds of the complex
- Relatively heavy-for-you kettlebells

Whereas if the goal were hypertrophy (i.e. muscle building) I would do something a little more like this:

- 2-6 exercises
- 8-12 reps per exercise
- 3 minutes rest between rounds of the complex
- Light to moderate kettlebells

And finally, if the goal is endurance:

- 2-6 exercises
- 15+ reps per exercise
- 1-2 minutes rest between rounds of the complex
- Light kettlebells

There is another option for endurance that involves a cousin of complexes, known as a chain, which involves doing a single rep of two or more exercises back-to-back and repeating it until you've done a certain amount of reps.

For example: 1 clean + 1 press.

THE KICK-ASS INSIDER'S GUIDE TO KETTLEBELL COMPLEXES

If you do (1 clean + 1 press) x 10, you've done 10 total cleans and 10 total presses.

Putting together multiple exercises like this has long been a secret weapon for sneaking in some serious conditioning while using strength movements as the catalyst for it all. Though it's been around for quite a long time, its lately been catapulted front and center in the kettlebell world by StrongFirst's Chief of Education Brett Jones with his *Iron Cardio* program.

While this approach might SEEM easier, in many ways it's far tougher, since you can't really get into much of a groove with an exercise as you're constantly transitioning between two or more drills, which in and of itself provides a great deal of added conditioning on top of the performance of the movements themselves.

#2: Number of Kettlebells

This doesn't refer just to the number of kettlebells you own, but rather to the number of kettlebells you're using in your complex. Obviously, your options are either 1 or 2. If you can figure out how to use 3 kettlebells, well…good on ya.

Now, you might just assume that more automatically equals better, and therefore 2 bells is what you should stick with no matter what, but you'd be surprised. You can get dynamite results in any of the categories – strength, hypertrophy, or endurance – with just one bell. And while I'd prefer you use two bells for the strength and hypertrophy complexes, you're definitely better off with one bell for endurance complexes.

Other reasons to use just one bell rather than two:

If you're a raw beginner. There are definitely movements even the bare-bones beginner can do with two kettlebells, but if doing a classic complex is your aim, you're much better off focusing on just one kettlebell until you get your technique down.

If your flexibility/mobility is not yet up to snuff. In this case, you'll DEFINITELY want to use just one bell – unless, of course, you are dead-set on buying your surgeon next year's model Mercedes. Then by all means show us all how big and strong you are, tough guy.

"But what if I don't have equal-sized kettlebells?" you may ask.

That's perfect. Just do uneven kettlebell complexes. To be quite honest, that is one of my favorite ways to lift double bells. The uneven (and thus unstable) nature of any lift using different-sized weights is immediately more challenging and seems to have even better carryover into real-world tasks. Don't knock it 'til you've tried it!

#3: The Flow, or The "Anti-Flow"

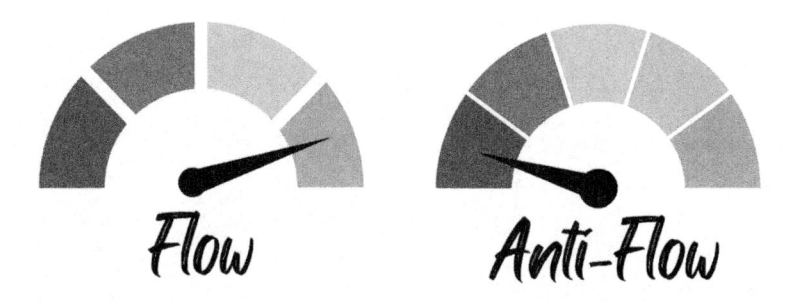

Flow   *Anti-Flow*

This is an element I rarely hear anyone talk about, but one that can help you make untold leaps in both your strength AND conditioning.

Kettlebell exercises can basically be broken into two broad categories:

Grinds (presses, rows, squats, etc)

Ballistics (swings, cleans, snatches, etc)

We can also break them down further into other categories, such as

Lower body (squat, lunge, swing)

Upper body (press, row, snatch)

Heck, let's go one step further:

Stable (squats, swings)

Less stable (Lunges, single leg deadlifts)

Now, the OBVIOUS approach – one that would occur to just about anyone putting together a complex – is to make the exercises flow nicely together.

ALEKS "THE HEBREW HAMMER" SALKIN

Ex: Clean, press, squat.

Clean   *Press*   *Squat*

Cleans normally precede and set up your presses, and squats are easy to put at the end of presses and cleans because your lower body is relatively fresh even if your upper body has gotten a little fatigued with the cleans and presses.

I'd argue that this arrangement – a well-flowing complex – is the most sensible approach in most cases. Think back to the point I made earlier about complexes being a very natural way to lift heavy objects in the real world: the benefits of seamlessly flowing from one movement to another to accomplish a task should be obvious. Why make things harder on yourself by putting the exercises in an order where the movements don't build on one another?

For strength and hypertrophy (muscle building) I'd suggest that you always "go for the flow."

Conditioning, however, is a little different.

THE KICK-ASS INSIDER'S GUIDE TO KETTLEBELL COMPLEXES

Let's take a look at a sample conditioning complex with a good flow:

	Exercises	Reps
A1	Swing	5
A2	Clean	5
A3	High Pull	5
A4	Snatch	5

One-arm swing   *Clean*   *High pull*   *Snatch*

With each rep you're slowly building up to elevating the bell more and more until it reaches the logical crescendo, and with each passing rep the momentum increases and makes doing the snatch easier than if you were to start just with snatches.

But if you're in the mood to make it tougher, you might break it up and do something like this:

	Exercises	**Reps**
A1	High Pull	5
A2	Clean	5
A3	Swing	5
A4	Snatch	5

ALEKS "THE HEBREW HAMMER" SALKIN

High pull    *Clean*    *One-arm swing*    *Snatch*

The changing degrees of elevation in this simple re-ordering of the moves can make it a MUCH tougher complex due to the 'broken up' nature of the flow – meaning that rather than progressively stacking the ballistic drills by the height to which the kettlebell goes (and thus the amount of power exerted when performing the movement), you're randomizing it, which makes it much more challenging. Try it if you don't believe me.

From my experience, this anti-flow in complexes makes for a great way to build what we in the kettlebell world like to call (or at least USED to like to call) *incidental conditioning* – that is, improvements in your conditioning despite the fact that you are working on something else. While you'll get it in abundance in both strength and hypertrophy complexes, learning how to increase the conditioning effect of endurance-focused complexes can help take your stamina and all-day strength to new and exciting levels you may never have thought possible.

THE KICK-ASS INSIDER'S GUIDE TO KETTLEBELL COMPLEXES

But again, I must repeat: when putting together your own strength or hypertrophy focused complexes, avoid anti-flow! If you're going heavy, the last thing you need is to make your life any harder than it has to be.

With that said, let's take a look at the program, the complexes, and more.

THE PROGRAMMING

The program will be based around a *Daily Undulating Periodization* model, where the focus will change from day to day: one day you'll go heavier (for strength), one day you'll use more moderate weights (hypertrophy), and yet another day you'll go light (for endurance).

Why Daily Undulating Periodization?

Without going into every conceivable detail about the benefits of D.U.P., let's just talk a little bit about the *la piece de resistance* of it:

The potential to get more gains, faster. All while still doing the same exercises.

And not just a little bit faster, either. According to some studies, you can potentially nearly DOUBLE your strength in the same period of time with Daily Undulating Periodization.

In one such study, the researchers set up two groups, both of which had at least 5 years of strength training under their belts:

> **Group #1**: Did a standard periodization protocol where each cycle they would increase the intensity (i.e. weight) of the exercises practiced - Weeks 1-4 were at 8 rep max (RM), weeks 5-8 were at 6RM, and weeks 9-12 were at 4RM (in other words, every 4 weeks the weight got heavier)

Group #2: Did the same exercises, but with daily undulating periodization

Day 1 at 8 rep max (RM), Day 2 at 6RM, and Day 3 at 4RM (in other words, every day a different level of intensity)

By the end of the program, here were the results

Improvement in bench press:

Standard periodization group: 14.4% increase

Daily Undulated Periodization group: 28.8% increase

Improvement in leg press:

Standard periodization group: 25.7% increase

Daily Undulated Periodization group: 55.8% increase

In conclusion:

Both approaches work - but one works faster.

It's really the difference between taking the highway and taking the scenic route in your strength results. Nothing wrong with the scenic route, but wouldn't you like to arrive at your destination almost twice as fast if given the chance?

The Takeaway:

The interplay of each of these types of complexes can ultimately lead to gains all around the board, and as the weeks go on all of them should start feeling easier.

The strength and hypertrophy days will follow the beat of a familiar drum using complexes as you've learned about them, and the endurance day will be focused on using a chain – again, a few exercises done back-to-back for one rep at a time, repeated for a desired number of total reps.

This will seem easy at first, but as the minutes pile on, so will the difficulty. Hear me now and believe me later.

Let's take an eagle's eye view at the workouts:

THE COMPLEXES

Strength Complex Day

Double KB row

Double KB clean

Double KB press

Double KB squat

Double KB swing

Hypertrophy Complex Day

Double KB clean   *Long Push Press (full squat into a press)*

Double KB row   *Double KB deadlift*

THE KICK-ASS INSIDER'S GUIDE TO KETTLEBELL COMPLEXES

Endurance Complex Day

Snatch *Squat* *Row*

Clean *Press* *Lunge*

Wanna get some quick swipe-and-deploy technique tips on all these moves? Get instant access to my FREE Video Resource Center here: www.KettlebellComplex.com

Or, point your smartphone's camera at this QR code and click the link that pops up:

ALEKS "THE HEBREW HAMMER" SALKIN

Now that you've gotten an eagle's eye view of the complexes, let's take a look at the Rules of Engagement for the program itself.

RULES OF ENGAGEMENT

"Smokey, this is not 'Nam...there are rules."

Walter Sobchak, The Big Lebowski

While the various types of complexes might have different nuances, they all play by a similar set of rules – namely that you want to use weights that are appropriate for you AND that you want to stay well within your abilities so that you can be challenged, but successful.

"Appropriate" in this context means we'll be using weights that correspond to a given ability level with your military press.

Why your press?

Because you can typically press less weight than you can do other movements, making them the "weak link" in the chain. If you choose your weights based on what you can do in a movement like squats, where you can almost certainly move heavier weights (at least I hope) you'll find that very quickly your presses either become unmanageable OR you have to scale back the number of reps you're doing with them.

Rules for strength complex:

- Use kettlebells that correspond to your 8-10 rep double pressing max.

- Aim for full-body tension throughout the grinds, maximum explosive power in the ballistics

Rules for the hypertrophy complex:

- Use kettlebells that correspond to roughly your 12-15 rep pressing max. This may necessitate that you use uneven kettlebells. If that's the case, just be sure to alternate which side the lighter and heavier kettlebell are on each round (ex: if on the first round the lighter bell is on your left side and heavier on your right, then in the second round make sure the left side takes the heavier bell and the right side takes the lighter bell)

- Resist the urge to set the kettlebells down prematurely!

- Though I would think long and hard before doing it, you CAN go a little heavier on this complex than just your 12-15 rep pressing max due to the fact that you're not technically doing a strict military press in this complex, but rather a long push press (deep squat immediately into a press where the momentum from the squat helps assist in the press). If you've got a decent amount of experience with kettlebells and are feeling froggy, then you can instead base this complex around a 12-15 rep squatting max instead. Just make sure your lats can keep up when it comes time for the rows!

Rules for the endurance complex:

- Use the same size bell you used for the hypertrophy day

- Pace yourself and aim to make your 6-move complex take at least 30 seconds to do, as you'll be going 30 seconds on, 30 seconds off. **This means 30 seconds of the complex on your left side, rest 30 seconds. 30 seconds of the complex on your right side, rest 30 seconds.**

- Due to the strictly timed pace of this complex, you might consider going a little lighter in the beginning and seeing how

THE KICK-ASS INSIDER'S GUIDE TO KETTLEBELL COMPLEXES

you fare for the time allotted to the workout. If you feel like it was too heavy, go lighter. If you felt like you just had a daunting but doable workout, then you've got the right weight for the task at hand.

Rules for ALL complexes:

- Remember: the goal is to do these as a COMPLEX – **not** a circuit. So unless you absolutely need to (i.e. for safety reasons or because you're just exhausted and really need to catch your breath), do NOT rest in between exercises; flow from one to the other without rest.

- If you are not yet competent with double kettlebell drills, or you don't have enough bells, then **just use just one kettlebell**. If using a single kettlebell, do the entire complex on one side THEN move onto the other (ex: do all the exercises on the left side, then repeat on the right side).

- If there is a kettlebell move you can't do, such as the snatch, simply leave it out and replace it with one you CAN do, even if it means repeating a movement.

Pretty straight forward, no?

Now, before you get started, you're gonna need to make sure your body is ready and rarin' to go to lift safely and effectively. So to kick off each workout, we're gonna do some *movement prep* – also known as a "warm up", to use the parlance of our times.

MOVEMENT: THE MISSING LINK AND '5TH ELEMENT' OF REAL-WORLD STRENGTH

Probably the single biggest disconnect in the world of fitness training is the importance of movement.

Now, you might be thinking *"uh, I'm pretty sure people know they have to MOVE in order to get fit!"* but that's not what I mean by movement; I'm not talking about merely "moving around" but rather the art and science of human movement.

Humans are easily the most unique organism on the face of the planet, with bodies versatile enough allow us to live in the arctic or in the tropics; to lift 1,000 lbs off the ground or run for 200 miles straight; to hold our breath for 5 minutes as we dive as deep as possible under water or climb to the top of the world's tallest mountains.

Each of us has within us a certain 'movement map' that lays down the foundation of the movements we are able to do. Think of it as our operating system. Just like a computer has a system for operating, so too does our body, and when it comes to movement, our body thinks in patterns.

So why do almost ZERO fitness professionals talk about this?

THE KICK-ASS INSIDER'S GUIDE TO KETTLEBELL COMPLEXES

Beats me!

But hear me out:

If you base your training on the quality of your movement in general and movement patterns in particular, you'll have a huge leg up on the speed and ease with which you can make massive gains in short order and will be light years ahead of your peers as they trudge along the hard way, eking out small amounts of progress over a long time, while you snag huge gains on your strength with lightning speed.

While there are a number of patterns we could talk about, for our purposes the most important ones that I want to begin with are the patterns that make up the foundation of ALL of our later movements:

The Original Strength RESETS

The Resets (a term coined and popularized by an organization called Original Strength) are based off the movements of the human developmental sequence. These reset patterns are:

- Diaphragmatic breathing
- Head control
- Rolling
- Rocking
- Gait pattern

These are all the movements that you begin to do sequentially as a baby, turning you into the walking, talking, running, and lifting person you are today.

These categories above contain a lot of different movements and variations within them, and as mentioned earlier, all of them lay the foundation for all the LATER movements you know and love (for our purposes, the traditional kettlebell and bodyweight movements). Without a solid foundation for movement, all your training will be like building a castle on sand.

Not only do the above movement patterns help you to successfully build yourself into a functional person as a child, but when revisited as an adult, they can help you to fortify and rejuvenate your natural body movements so you can more easily build yourself up to the level of strength and power you were made to have.

THE KICK-ASS INSIDER'S GUIDE TO KETTLEBELL COMPLEXES

Deep breathing

Neck nods

Rolling

Rocking

Crawling

All told, these movements will get your body to move the way it was MADE to move.

ALEKS "THE HEBREW HAMMER" SALKIN

The more your body moves the way it was made to move, the more you'll be able to move your body the way you want to move – for greater strength, muscle, stamina, and resilience.

The less your body moves the way it was made to move, the more modifications, exercise substitutions, and frustrating complexity you'll have to introduce to your training. To me, the choice is obvious. Want simple, effective, and time-efficient workouts? Get back in touch with your most foundational of movement patterns!

Want frustration, fits and starts, and mediocre results? Ignore your movement foundation and simply try to force your body to do the things it's not yet ready for.

Either way, the choice is yours, but I know which option I'm picking!

THE KICK-ASS INSIDER'S GUIDE TO KETTLEBELL COMPLEXES

Stretching and Mobility

Like it or not, as we get up in years, it becomes more and more apparent that "use it or lose it" is practically an iron-clad law of the universe. If you do not utilize your body's natural mobility and flexibility, your body will adapt to the ranges of motion you use most often, even if they're not in your best interest.

I view movement improvement as equivalent to filling in the pot holes, shaving down the speed bumps, and knocking down the road blocks in advance of your journey so you can expect a much smoother ride. You often don't know when you'll encounter "hiccups" in your training, but you can give yourself a fighting chance by treating your *movability* (as I like to call it) as seriously as you treat your strength.

First up is Y pulses.

These are a great drill for opening up your thoracic spine, specifically helping it to extend better – of big-time importance for all overhead lifting work, something kettlebells specialize in.

ALEKS "THE HEBREW HAMMER" SALKIN

Instructions:

- Open your chest wide (imagine you are spreading the logo on your shirt) and put your hands up in the 'Y' position.
- Keep a light brace in your abs (don't let your butt try to escape behind you!) lean up against a sturdy wall with your hands and push your chest toward the wall in little pulsations. Go back and forth an inch or so at a time.
- Keep your thumbs pointed behind you.
- **Number of pulses per set:** 10-20
- **Number of sets:** 1-3

THE KICK-ASS INSIDER'S GUIDE TO KETTLEBELL COMPLEXES

Chair Twists

Another excellent move for upper body mobility and flexibility is the chair twist. As the name implies, you use a chair to help you twist your body – excellent not just for an out-of-this-world stretch, but also for helping to mobilize and 'bulletproof' your spine.

Here's how to do them:

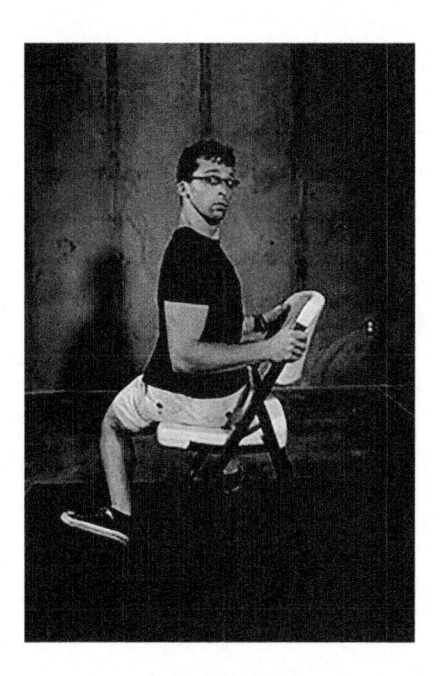

Instructions

- Find a sturdy chair and sit in it sideways. Once again, "spread the logo on your shirt" to maintain a big chest.
- Using your hands, gently pull yourself into a twisted position. Be sure to keep a big chest (do NOT hunch over!) and strive to look over the shoulder on the side where you're twisting.

- Pull with one hand and push with the other. You will want to pull on the side to which you are twisting, and push on the side where you are resisting.

  For example, in the above picture, I am twisting to my right side, so I am pulling with my right arm and pushing with my left to increase the stretch.

  Again, do this gently. If you have not twisted in a while, a little will go a long way.

- **Hold time:** however long it takes to take in 5-10 slow, deep breaths. Then switch sides and repeat. Do this 1-3 times per side.

Hanging

The benefits of hanging are so long and so numerous that I just can't do it justice here. I have an entire 28-day challenge called *Hanguary* (originally released in January, hence the name) that dives deep into the benefits as well as practical applications of hanging, but for now suffice it to say that the big thing you're likely to get out of it as a kettlebell enthusiast is the fact that it can help you:

- Soothe your shoulders
- Increase your overhead mobility
- Strengthen your grip
- Decompress your spine

And much, much more. Here's how to do 'em:

THE KICK-ASS INSIDER'S GUIDE TO KETTLEBELL COMPLEXES

- Grab onto a sturdy overhanging implement such as a pullup bar, rings, or even a ledge of some sort (provided you don't end up dangling precariously like Sylverster Stallone in *Cliffhanger*)
- Unless you hate the hell out of your shoulders and prefer that they hurt 24/7, you MUST keep your elbows straight. This doesn't mean aggressively locked out, just straightened; do not hang with a notable or intentional bend in your elbows.
- If you find you have TIGHT shoulders, you may want to go with passive hangs (letting your shoulders shrug up toward your ears).
- If you have LOOSE shoulders, you should stick with active hangs (sucking your shoulders into your sockets)

Quad Stretches

Believe it or not, getting someone to stretch their quads seriously for the first time often requires NOT some of the more advanced stretches, but the simplest ones done PROPERLY.

ALEKS "THE HEBREW HAMMER" SALKIN

I've seen a lot of people do this stretch, but I doubt I've seen 1 in 1,000 (save for my own students, of course) do it effectively. I'll fix that.

Start position   *End position*

- Grab onto a sturdy surface with your free hand, and grab the instep of your opposite foot

- Tuck your tail under (imagine you're pointing your belt buckle toward your nose) and try to pull your heel toward your glute. It may not make it the whole way; just go as far as you can without excessive discomfort. Similarly, keep the knee of the bent leg right next to that of the grounded leg. Don't let it migrate forward! You will kill the stretch.

- Once you've gotten into position, the next step is to actively dorsiflex your ankle – i.e. try to pull your toes down toward the ground (see the pictures above). Make sure you offer some resistance with your hand, and do NOT let your knee come forward or relax your quad in any way. That will make you lose the effectiveness of the stretch. Keep your knee in line with your grounded leg.

- Hold the position for 20-30 seconds, aiming to pick up some 'slack' and increase your range of motion whenever possible. Repeat on the other leg.
- *Complete 1-3 rounds per leg.*

Hamstring Stretches

RDL Hamstring stretch

Hamstrings are another perennial pain in the you-know-what to a great many people. And while there are a lot of great hamstring stretches out there, I figured, why not rely on one that gets you MAD gains super fast using a movement you're already more or less familiar with: the deadlift?

In this case, we're going to be using the Romanian deadlift - a variation that involves very little knee bend but very strong hip bend. This will light up your hamstrings and pry them open like a can of figurative sardines, too.

To do these:

- *Grab a light kettlebell (or two) and deadlift them normally.*

- *Push your butt back and bend your knees only very slightly - roughly 50% of what you'd normally do for a deadlift (note: the bells will almost certainly NOT touch the ground. Look at the picture above. I am more flexible than the average guy, and even I cannot get them to touch the ground while maintaining a neutral spine position. Once you feel the stretch, you've gone far enough!)*

- *Pause at the bottom position for 10-15 seconds, squeeze the hamstrings and glutes as hard as you can (brace as though someone were going to kick you), and then relax, picking up the slack in the muscle and lowering slightly further from the hinge in your hips. Do NOT bend at the low back to get more range of motion – the only movement should be in the hamstrings/hips! Rest briefly at the bottom position, then stand back up.*

- *Do this 1-3 times*

Eagle's Eye View

Here's a quick bird's eye view of what your training is going to look like for the next several weeks.

You will start with your movement prep (below) and then immediately start your workout. And in the spirit of this book on complexes, I thought, why not put the warm up into a complex as well? How clever.

THE KICK-ASS INSIDER'S GUIDE TO KETTLEBELL COMPLEXES

You'll start off with the Original Strength resets:

	Reset	Duration/Reps
A1	Deep Breathing	1 minute
A2	Neck Nods	10 up and down, 10 over each shoulder
A3	Rolling	5 in each direction
A4	Rocking	20 reps
A5	Crawling	1 minutes

Do 1 round

You'll then follow them up with these stretches:

	Reset	Duration/Reps
B1	Y-Pulses	10-20
B2	Chair Twists	Hold for 5-10 breaths in each direction
B3	Hanging	20-30 seconds
B4	Quad stretch	20-30 seconds per leg
B5	RDL Hamstring Stretch	10-15 seconds hold @ bottom position

Do 1 Round

Once you've done this, you can begin the workout of the day.

Before we begin, let me paraphrase the words of the great Ron Swanson from *Parks and Recreation*:

"I fear what you just read was, 'do the resets and stretches if you feel like it.' What I wrote was, do the resets and stretches before each workout."

I cannot stress this enough: most of us live very sedentary lives and do not move nearly as well or as naturally as we did when we were kids, or as well as we very easily could now with a little practice.

Do not skip the movement prep. If you are not doing the movement prep, you are not doing the program – you are doing your own incomplete version of the program, and therefore can't complain if you don't get the results you were hoping for. So no funny business, bucko.

In fact, I would go one step further and say that you should even do the warm up on your off days if for no other reason than to give yourself a running head start in improving your overall movement while also giving you a chance to shake some of the soreness off of your Soft Machine (your body) and instill better daily movement habits.

Wanna see these moves in action to make sure you're getting the most out of them?

Join the free Video Resource Center here: *www.KettlebellComplex.com*

Or, point your smartphone's camera at this QR code and click the link that pops up:

BEFORE YOU BEGIN...

If you don't know where you are right now, it'll be pretty dang hard to see how far you've come once this program is over. So let's take a few measurements, shall we?

1. **For starters, get a few measurements of relevant kettlebell and bodyweight strength.**

   You already know which size of kettlebells to use for your complexes based on the rep maxes you'll need to shoot for in each category, but I always like to see the impact of a training program above and beyond just the weights you begin with.

   Here are a few suggestions:

   - **Number of swings or snatches you can do in 5 minutes a moderate kettlebell.**
   - **Number of front squats you can do with a pair of heavy-for-you kettlebells (or number of goblet squats you can do with your heaviest kettlebell)**
   - **Number of strict pullups**. If you can't do any pullups, test how long you can do the dead hang or flexed arm hang.
   - **Number of strict pushups**
   - **How long or far you can carry your heaviest kettlebell or pair of kettlebells.**

Feel free to add anything else you might want to test – the choices are endless.

2. **Get some health measurements as well.**

   At a minimum I'd suggest the following:

   - Waistline
   - Resting heart rate

   Other valuable ones would be what you look like in the mirror (take pictures for this – our memories tend to deceive us), scale weight, and so on. Apart from the resting heart rate one, I credit Josh Hillis and Dan John for these measurements from their book *Fat Loss Happens on Monday*, because let's face it: most of us could stand to lose a little weight, and even if we're not actively trying to, it's nice to be able to look in the mirror and see a new and improved you.

   Get it? Got it? Good. With that said, let's take a look at your program for the next four weeks.

Week 1

Day 1: Strength complex

	Exercise	Reps
A1	Double kettlebell row	3
A2	Double kettlebell clean	3
A3	Double kettlebell press	3
A4	Double kettlebell squat	3
A5	Double kettlebell swing	3

Complete 5 total rounds – rest 3 minutes between rounds

Day 2: Hypertrophy complex

	Exercise	Reps
A1	Double kettlebell clean	8
A2	Double kettlebell long push press	8
A3	Double kettlebell row	8
A4	Double kettlebell deadlift	8

Complete 3 total rounds – rest 3 minutes between rounds

Day 3: Endurance complex (1 kettlebell only)

	Exercise	Reps
A1	Snatch	1
A2	Squat	1
A3	Row	1
A4	Clean	1
A5	Press	1
A6	Lunge	1

Minute 1: 1 round, right side. Minute 2: 1 round, left side. Repeat this cycle for 16 minutes

Week 2

Day 1: Strength complex

	Exercise	Reps
A1	Double kettlebell row	4
A2	Double kettlebell clean	4
A3	Double kettlebell press	4
A4	Double kettlebell squat	4
A5	Double kettlebell swing	4

Complete 5 total rounds – rest 3 minutes between rounds

Day 2: Hypertrophy complex

	Exercise	Reps
A1	Double kettlebell clean	10
A2	Double kettlebell long push press	10
A3	Double kettlebell row	10
A4	Double kettlebell deadlift	10

Complete 3 total rounds – rest 3 minutes between rounds

Day 3: Endurance complex (1 kettlebell only)

	Exercise	Reps
A1	Snatch	1
A2	Squat	1
A3	Row	1
A4	Clean	1
A5	Press	1
A6	Lunge	1

Minute 1: 1 round, right side. Minute 2: 1 round, left side. Repeat this cycle for 20 minutes.

Week 3

Day 1: Strength complex

	Exercise	Reps
A1	Double kettlebell row	5
A2	Double kettlebell clean	5
A3	Double kettlebell press	5
A4	Double kettlebell squat	5
A5	Double kettlebell swing	5

Complete 5 total rounds – rest 3 minutes between rounds

Day 2: Hypertrophy complex

	Exercise	Reps
A1	Double kettlebell clean	12
A2	Double kettlebell long push press	12
A3	Double kettlebell row	12
A4	Double kettlebell deadlift	12

Complete 3 total rounds – rest 3 minutes between rounds

Day 3: Endurance complex (1 kettlebell only)

	Exercise	Reps
A1	Snatch	1
A2	Squat	1
A3	Row	1
A4	Clean	1
A5	Press	1
A6	Lunge	1

Minute 1: 1 round, right side. Minute 2: 1 round, left side. Repeat this cycle for 24 minutes

Week 4 – BACK OFF WEEK

Day 1: Strength complex

	Exercise	Reps
A1	Double kettlebell row	3
A2	Double kettlebell clean	3
A3	Double kettlebell press	3
A4	Double kettlebell squat	3
A5	Double kettlebell swing	3

Complete 3 total rounds – rest 3 minutes between rounds

Day 2: Hypertrophy complex

	Exercise	Reps
A1	Double kettlebell clean	6
A2	Double kettlebell long push press	6
A3	Double kettlebell row	6
A4	Double kettlebell deadlift	6

Complete 3 total rounds – rest 3 minutes between rounds

Day 3: Endurance complex (1 kettlebell only)

	Exercise	Reps
A1	Snatch	1
A2	Squat	1
A3	Row	1
A4	Clean	1
A5	Press	1
A6	Lunge	1

Minute 1: 1 round, right side. Minute 2: 1 round, left side. Repeat this cycle for 12 minutes

Week 5

Once week 5 rolls around, I want you to take a few days off and rest up. That means:

- Eat a little more
- Sleep a little more
- Keep up your stretching, mobility, and movement regimen

And on a day when you're feeling pretty fresh and well recovered, you'll put a few things to the test.

Warm up well, then get to testing!

- If you feel so inclined, re-test your previous maxes in your kettlebell press for the strength and hypertrophy complexes (your 8-10 rep max and 12-15 rep max respectively). Alternatively, you might just pick up a heavier pair of kettlebells (or a heavier single kettlebell) and just see what you can get away with in the press.

Once you've done that, test the moves you did at the beginning of the program (including any movements you tested not on the list below)

  - **Number of swings or snatches you can do in 5 minutes with a moderate kettlebell.**
  - **Number of front squats you can do with a pair of heavy-for-you kettlebells (or number of goblet squats you can do with your heaviest kettlebell)**
  - **Number of strict pullups.** If you can't do any pullups, test how long you can do the dead hang or flexed arm hang.

- **Number of strict pushups**
- **How long or far you can carry your heaviest kettlebell or pair of kettlebells.**

How did you fare?

If you followed the program to the letter, I'm betting you did pretty darn well.

So there you have it!

The kick-ass insider's guide to kettlebell complexes.

Maybe you're surprised that this guide wasn't a little more...*complex* (see what I did there?)

Well, you're in luck, friend-o; it ain't. Like with most things, kettlebell complexes distill down into certain iron-clad principles, practices, and strategies – and once you know them and know how to apply them, you can start putting together some serious, solid complexes to increase your strength, muscle, power, and endurance in no time flat.

Give this 4-week program a shot any time you're in need of a quantum leap in your training and see if you don't continually make some huge leaps forward. And if you use these principles to put together your own complexes, feel free to drop me a line and let me know what you've come up with; I'd love to see it.

And if you haven't already, don't forget to take advantage of the FREE Video Resource Center at *www.KettlebellComplex.com*

Or, point your smartphone's camera at this QR code and click the link that pops up:

THE KICK-ASS INSIDER'S GUIDE TO KETTLEBELL COMPLEXES

ALEKS "THE HEBREW HAMMER" SALKIN

And if you're eager to take your kettlebell skills to the next level, be sure to reach out about 1-on-1 coaching with Yours Jewly (i.e. me) so you can eliminate your speed bumps and road blocks and soar to new and exciting heights of raw strength and brute power in short order. Details on the next few pages.

Have fun and happy training!

Aleks "The Hebrew Hammer" Salkin

Aleks "The Hebrew Hammer" Salkin is a level 2 StrongFirst certified kettlebell instructor (SFG II) and an Original Strength Instructor.

He grew up scrawny, unathletic, weak, and goofy until he was exposed to kettlebells and the teaching and methodology of Pavel in his early 20s, and took his training and movement skills to the next level upon discovering Original Strength in his mid-20s. He is currently based out of Omaha, Nebraska where he spends his time spreading the word of strength, movement, and healthy living.

ALEKS "THE HEBREW HAMMER" SALKIN

He is the author of the smash hit best seller The No BS Kettlebell and Bodyweight Kickstart Program as well as the now world-famous 9-Minute Kettlebell and Bodyweight Challenge. Find him online at www.alekssalkin.com

TRAIN AND GAIN WITH ALEKS

When it comes to improving their strength and fitness, many men are content to play the pioneer, grabbing their proverbial machete and slashing their way through the veritable jungle of complicated, conflicting, and sometimes contradictory advice on how to go from the quaint, provincial village they've long found themselves stuck in to the hidden City of Gold – the place where the truest version of themselves lays in wait to be finally unleashed; the version brimming with raw strength, brute power, endless athleticism, and seemingly superhuman resilience – and all the internal and external confidence that goes along with it, radiating outward for all to immediately detect and respect.

Reaching this tucked-away metropolis is the strength and fitness equivalent of discovering the New World.

It's an exciting path.

However, it is often a slow one, replete with sand traps, dead ends, and creeping and slithering perils that lurk around every corner, waiting to pounce on you with one wrong move.

Many relish the opportunity to grab a map – that is, a course, program, or challenge – and boldly strike out on their own, with the journey in search of this city being half the fun. And given that

I have written out many such "maps" throughout the years, there are no shortage of self-guided paths out there for the enterprising strength and movement enthusiast.

More:

There are fewer slings and arrows to suffer – but ultimately YOU must guide your path and navigate any unforeseen snags and setbacks that may unexpectedly rear their heads.

Another option?

Hire an expert guide to lead the way for you – and AVOID the most common frustrations, setbacks, and unpleasant surprises that lurk around every corner!

THE KICK-ASS INSIDER'S GUIDE TO KETTLEBELL COMPLEXES

If you're interested in learning more about consulting or coaching with me, reach out via email at aleks@alekssalkin.com with the subject line "coaching" and we'll talk.

ALEKS "THE HEBREW HAMMER" SALKIN

In the meantime, take a moment to read about the dazzling transformations of your fellow hard-charging kettlebell and calisthenics fanatics who took the plunge and conquered the obstacles that laid in their path...

ALL GAIN, NO PAIN!

Australia's First Iron Maiden Soars to New Heights of Pullup Power with Programming from the Hebrew Hammer

Back in 2018 my training was on a slow burn. I had started to get tendinitis in my elbows and my stubborn self had set a goal to achieve something few people ever have: a pullup with an extra 36 kg of weight strapped to me (in my case, a full 60% of my bodyweight).

Things were looking grim, as not only would the weight not budge, but every time I did weighted pullups, my elbows would scream at me, forcing me to stick to bodyweight-only pullups.

I reached out to Aleks to ask if he'd be willing to take me on as a student, and shortly after things started to change dramatically.

He did a full-on deep dive into my training history, pinpointed my weaknesses and the gaps in my development, and using his knowledge of a variety of modalities and old-school training

ALEKS "THE HEBREW HAMMER" SALKIN

*principles and practices, crafted together a program that not only smoothed out all of my rough spots, but ultimately got me to a downright EASY 36 kg pullup with **NO elbow pain**! Best of all, he is encouraging, witty, and makes the process of training for such daunting goals exciting rather than borderline clinical. Highly recommended!*

Frances Moylan

"The Movement Maker", Perth, Australia

THE KICK-ASS INSIDER'S GUIDE TO KETTLEBELL COMPLEXES

From "Overtrained and Injured" to EASILY Dominating StrongFirst's Level 2 Kettlebell Certification

"I was embarking upon my StrongFirst SFG2 re-certification and needed to start training. I sought out Aleks on Instagram and contacted him to see if he would be willing to help me out. My first impression was very positive. He was prompt in his response and was helpful right off the bat.

In the past, I was overtrained and injured by the time I got to certification weekend. I needed a new approach to my training. Aleks offered a way to achieve my goals. A simple program to follow to avoid burning myself out. He took into consideration how I live my life day to day, i.e. very active and a lot of use to my upper body. No other coaches have ever taken my every day activity into consideration when programming a training plan. I needed quick and effective sessions and to be able to do everything I needed to do in 3 sessions per week. Aleks was able to offer me just that, in a balanced, smart way.

Following Aleks' templates, I passed my SFG2 re-certification with far more ease than any other certification. I was even given high praise by my Master instructor and teammates. If you're looking for a coach to help you train smarter, not harder, Aleks is the guy! I highly recommend him to help you reach your goals."

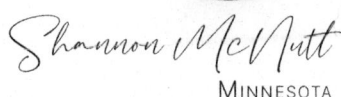

Shannon McNutt
MINNESOTA

ALEKS "THE HEBREW HAMMER" SALKIN

An Eastern Medicine Practitioner Raves:

"I can honestly say that without you, I'd be a less effective health practitioner."

Aleks :) Hope you're well, my friend!

Now, at the risk of changing tone drastically lol, please answer honestly, and I promise I'll repeat it to no-one, if that's required by the US legal system :-p ... I wonder if you could tell me, how much / how often, you treat "serious stuff"? Y'know: frozen shoulders... slipped discs... "surgery-level" stuff.

As you know, I'm an Eastern Medicine practitioner - i.e., acupuncturist and herbalist - and crawling, neck nods, YTWLs, and other methods/techniques I've learnt from you have become a mainstay in my practice.

I don't say this lightly, and I hope my tone carries over email: the effectiveness of these drills cuts into my bottom line, and I mean that in a GREAT way! Once I've been able to reduce a patient's level of inflammation to the point where regular, gentle movements are appropriate, RESETs and - if you'll allow the term - other Salkinesque "move how your body is meant to move"-type drills pay fantastic dividends. Yesterday, I had a patient who doesn't attend a gym buy her 15lb kitty litter one week ahead, so she'll always have something on hand to do carries and rehab her shoulder.

For the good of my own clients, I'd love to hear more about what you're working with, but either way, be proud of yourself today, my friend! Your hilarious, gripping emails, YT and social media posts

THE KICK-ASS INSIDER'S GUIDE TO KETTLEBELL COMPLEXES

are genuinely motivating, and having now prescribed OS RESETs to clients for over three years, I can honestly say that without you, I'd be a less effective health practitioner.

Best,

Felix Niland

SYDNEY, AUSTRALIA

ALEKS "THE HEBREW HAMMER" SALKIN

United States Marine Veteran Gets Back into Fighting Spirit with The Hebrew Hammer's Mad Methods!

Aleks,

I did the exact resets we identified as working best for me, then after the crawl I added a backward crawl.

Right after that, just for kicks, I went to the pullup bar - and to my surprised knocked out a perfect rep! Something about the exact resets you helped me identify + tossing in the backward crawl = magic. Amazing stuff.

Thank you!

Stu Greenbaum

"The Flexible Steel Ankle Openers from Strongevity were a revelation. After performing just one set of each, I felt an immediate and significant increase in my hip and t-spine mobility, especially rotationally. And at my chiropractor appointment that evening, my doc commented that he had not felt my spine move so well in years. Another win from Aleks - thank you for helping to keep me young and strong!"

Stu Greenbaum

THE KICK-ASS INSIDER'S GUIDE TO KETTLEBELL COMPLEXES

"My wife swears I'm the best looking I've ever been"

Hi Aleks,

Just got back from vacation in FL. I have to say thank you. This is really the first time in years that I've felt confident with my shirt off at the beach. Not that I was the most jacked guy at the beach, but I at least looked like a man who does front squats and handstands and that's pretty damn good!

[...]after my first son was born 5 years ago I definitely slipped into dad bod. And in the last 8 months we've been working together I feel and look the best since I can remember. My wife swears I'm the best looking I've ever been.

I tack on your kb and bodyweight challenge to most strength workouts. I deadbug daily and do the os resets you taught me almost daily.

I know you're supposed to say that "I did all the work" or something like that but you coached me on what I need to work on and how to progress and I really cannot thank you enough.

My dad was never comfortable enough to take his shirt off at the pool or beach. Always wearing a shirt and I always thought that was weird. I felt proud as a father to set a good example of health and fitness for my kids at the beach.

Josh Boccheciamp

ALEKS "THE HEBREW HAMMER" SALKIN

More great progress from Josh:

Hi Aleks,

Some good news-

I did 10 dips with the 24 kg bell attached. That's a PR

I did 4 chinups with the 24kg bell attached. That's a PR.

In both cases, I had a little more in the tank.

I overhand deadlifted 345 which is the most weight I have and the most I've done since I can remember. An adult PR if you will.

--

Somethings I've noticed through the first two weeks. All aches and pains in my body are basically gone. The upper body segmental role I think was magic at calming down my laps and the little muscles behind my armpits. Squat depth is at my all time best. My heels are only coming up a little on the air squat, and I've been squating with a dowl overhead. I'm sleeping sound on my back too with my arms overhead. I've noticed that I've been internally rotating my shoulders when I sleep, probably for years. All good things.

The 40-Year-Old Surgeon Nails His First Muscle Up

Hey Aleks!

Wanted to give you a break-down of my progress so far. I started my muscle up journey after a consultation and plan with you on 11/13 to try and get a strict muscle up by 1/16 (turning 40). My baseline was 8 pullups and 10 dips at body weight. I had never done weighted pull ups or dips. I was able to meet my goal early on 1/4 based on your awesome plan. I gained some excellent strength in the process. Today, W8D3, I was able to knock out 4 single muscle ups (1r x4) which was pretty badass. Your plan pushed my limits, but I never had any injury concerns or needed to take a break besides COVID for a week, and extra recovery times due to lots of skiing and family. Oh and did I mention after our consultation session I've been able to do a nearly full back bridge?

I'm going to switch plans for a few months of calisthenics base building, but I'm sure to come back when I want some help with future goals of handstand and HSPU.

Thanks!

Dr. Judson Corn

More PRs and Progress Reports from the Good Doctor:

Yesterday I ran my first 1/2 marathon, which happened to be on a trail and happened to have 3200ft (1000m) of climbing in it, so not your average race. I started working with Aleks a little over a year ago after getting bored and not seeing results with minimalist kettlebell programs for the previous 8 years or so.

At first, all of those programs were great but then I slowly hit a plateau and jumped between minimalist programs but never got over that plateau.

My goals have always been to feel good, move well, and play in the mountains that I love. I've never been able to build up to much running without being in constant pain, especially my ankle and right IT band/hip.

I was able to revamp my backcountry skiing this year, and climbed over 60,000ft without pain. I was able to jump back into running PAIN FREE and just completed my first 1/2 marathon. You could say those goals are now being met!

Thanks, Aleks for all the great IC [Inner Circle – A.S.] programming, challenges, and encouragement!

THE KICK-ASS INSIDER'S GUIDE TO KETTLEBELL COMPLEXES

The Doctor gives his diagnosis of standard kettlebell programming vs. Hebrew Hammer kettlebell programming:

Well I tried to go back to some standard KB programming, you know, the single type movements repeated over and over? Yeah I made it one day.

Aleks has got me so far over the last year working on variety and especially body weight movements that have gotten me feeling wonderful, supple, and strong and also I have already gotten my biggest backcountry ski year in (50,000 ft of climbing and still going) without pain and enough confidence and single leg work to attack a trail 1/2 marathon in June (13 miles and 3400ft of climbing) for which I am doing multiple runs per week from not much running only needing a little extra hip work to be pain free.

A 50-Something School Teacher Achieves

The Testosterone Levels of a 19-year-old!

Hey Aleks, things are going really well. Deadlifts are coming along, I'm doing unilateral overhead press work for my shoulder injury (finally saw a PT for that) and still putting on muscle. I went to the doctor and my blood work came back fantastic. I have the testosterone of a healthy, non-obese male between the ages of 19 and 39, and my a1c has stabilized from 5.7 last year (pre-diabetic) to 5.5 (normal). All great news! Your advice has worked wonders.

Mark Manning

> **"I keep asking my wife to feel my butt because the results are great."**

Hey Aleks,

Okay we're down to one week left! Can't believe it went that fast. I wanted to check in with you briefly for some feedback and to ask questions about the next steps.

First and foremost, thank you, and holy shit this did work really well. I definitely put on about 3-4 lb of noticeable muscle, and overall feel stronger in the posterior chain as well as feeling the 'linkage' that I believe you were after with the crawls and carries.

Some comments:

Block 1: I just started doing barbell work again this week. With a disk injury 7 weeks ago and knee arthritis/torn meniscus, I felt NO pain squatting 2 × 5 with 95 lb. I know that's a low weight and low volume but the fact that it was pain-free was noteworthy. I'm going to try deadlifts tonight.

THE KICK-ASS INSIDER'S GUIDE TO KETTLEBELL COMPLEXES

Block 2: I fell in love with it in the latter part of the program. I'd actually love to keep the elevated pushups and seated rows because of how much I'm getting out of it. My hamstrings could probably use a few weeks off! My glutes are the biggest holy shit factor of all. I feel like my glutes get out of bed before the rest of me, and I keep asking my wife to feel my butt because the results are great. Remember the movie "How Stella Got Her Groove Back"? This is like how Mark got his glutes back.

Mark Manning

ALEKS "THE HEBREW HAMMER" SALKIN

Brick Layer raves:

"It has been at least a decade since my shoulders would allow me to do that and have no pain at the end of the day"

I wanted to let you know that the increased shoulder and back work you suggested is paying off. Today I was able to lay 12inch concrete block with one hand again. I has been at least a decade since my shoulders would allow me to do that and have no pain at the end of the day. Thanks for the help in getting back to a place where I can set a physical example for the young guys on the job, and not just yammer on about what I could do when I was their age.

Hazen Alward

Check out his other updates as well:

First I want to tell you that the addition of hip thrusts and the dumbell leg curls have done wonders for my left knee. Almost all of the lingering pain from the quad injury I had in November is gone now. I am very excited about this as I have done a lot to minimize the pain since the injury, but it kept coming back. Those two movements are the only thing I really changed, and they have been a huge benefit. Thanks

--

Good Morning Aleks. I hope that this finds you well.

I wanted to let you know that progress is being made, and I am pretty happy with it. I am almost at 2 sets of 5 with all of my Easy Strength movements that I am using this past round. The accessory lifts that you have given me to do are making a difference in my knees and shoulders as you predicted. I was able to take some beginners kayaking this past weekend, and spend almost 4 hours in my whitewater boat and paddle about 4 miles of flatwater, which is no mean feat in a whitewater boat that is not meant to go straight. I was a bit sore Sunday, but was good to go for training on Monday. This paddling trip was a great indicator for me that the path you have me on is a great one. In the past a trip like that would have had me beat up for days. It just makes it better that the folks that I took boating are less than half my age, but suffered more physical discomfort. Trip two is planned for this weekend so at least it was not to much for them.

--

Hello Aleks.

Wanted to let you know that I am sneaking up the goals I have. I was feeling good yesterday when I started training so I decided to warm up with moderate weight clean and jerks and snatches for a change from swings. I figured I had probably done enough in the 90 degree head to be pretty much ready to go after work. The 24 Kg snatches felt so good I went for a set of 28kg snatches for 10. That would not have been possible last year. Now I was feeling curious so I thought I would try the 32kg for snatches, which I had never successfully done before. The first one with my weak arm felt easy enough to continue so I knocked out 5 with each arm. This is not something I could have done before, and I was just warming up so I did not push anywhere near max.

I have intentionally not doing any near max training and hoping to just learn to trust the process. This one session proved unquestionably

ALEKS "THE HEBREW HAMMER" SALKIN

that what we are doing is working. Thank you for helping me plan out what I need to do and for helping me fill in my gaps. I am very happy with how I am progressing

--

I decided on a whim to attempt a 40 kg clean yesterday. I have never cleaned a bell of that size before so when it went up on each side I was pretty happy. I tried sets of 5 after that and succeeded. After that I tried snatching it, and was successful on my left side.

I was unable to press it on either side, but it was pretty cool to find out I could go that heavy on a whim.

THE KICK-ASS INSIDER'S GUIDE TO KETTLEBELL COMPLEXES

"I'm now convinced that my shoulder is largely healthy"

Hi Aleks,

Quick update:

I'm loving the exercises you showed me. I've never done exercises specifically targeted at the upper back and the shoulder blade muscles. So although I only use my body weight or extremely light weights, my upper back still gets sore. The pain I experienced when doing pull-ups is dissipating, and after two weeks of hanging actively, I can now hang passively.

You know I created this spreadsheet that's jam-packed with exercises and to be honest, in the beginning, I didn't do them all—mostly for time reasons. I often skipped the hip bridges during the S&S warmup, the marching and crawling parts of your 9-Minute Challenge, and runs were few and far between. However, I'm doing more every day and I made sure to always do the exercises you showed me.

There's one thing I have to confess, Aleks: Although you told me to not do any presses, I couldn't resist. I had to see if I'm progressing and attempted to press the 24kg bell with my injured hand. And I pulled it off! Also, I did my first Turkish get-up with the 32kg bell since the injury.

I'm now convinced that my shoulder is largely healthy. Otherwise, I wouldn't be able to perform a get-up with 32kg. After all, during the TGU you put a shoulder through its full range of motion with a substantial weight.

Yannick Hallas

Woman With Severe Rheumatoid Arthritis Regains Her Strength, Mobility, and Hope

Hi Aleks!

How are you? I hope you are great! I am Gabriela, the Uruguayan who lives in Germany and is married to Marcus. Do you remember me?

We had a coaching session three weeks ago and I want to tell you about my process.

First of all I want to thank you very much for all your work. Although I am not familiar with everything you do, since Marcus is the one who trains according to your methodology, I must say that the OS RESET exercises had and continue to have a transformative effect on my body, mind and spirit. They have not only given me back physical mobility, but also the HOPE of regaining control of my body's movements.

Approximately 2 months ago, I could not go down the stairs normally because my physical condition (Rheumatoid Arthritis) did not allow it. My knees and ankles hurt too much to bend. I also had no muscles in my legs because since I couldn't practically bend my knees, it was difficult for me to exercise my leg muscles.

Movement in my shoulders was also very limited. I couldn't fully raise my arms. So my husband, Marcus, told me to try the OS RESET exercises, obviously the ones I could.

At that time, I could only do dead back and neck nodding. Incredibly, after 1 week of practicing these exercises I started to walk better and raise my arms a little better too. After a month, my body asked me for more movement. It was as if an inner force had awakened in me and began to transform me.

THE KICK-ASS INSIDER'S GUIDE TO KETTLEBELL COMPLEXES

That's why we decided to have the coaching session with you and luckily you accepted! This is the third week since our session and every day I feel better. I must say that at the beginning it was challenging. Especially, the exercises with the arms, the upper body segmental roll and also the Command Crawling!

Off the record, the first week after doing these exercises I ended up crying! I think it was not only because my body began to rearrange itself, but possibly also because emotions encapsulated in those rigid and limited positions that I could do were released.

The first week I was able to do the exercises three days, the second four and this third week, five days in a row! I am happy because every day I see my progress. My legs begin to strengthen, my muscles begin to gain mass, my arms rise a little more every day.

Yes, I still have pain but it's a pain from rearrangement!

So dear Aleks, thank you so much for this gift and ability that you share with all of us! I hope that many people can benefit like me from these wonderful and healing techniques that you share with the world. And I hope that many people with physical conditions know you and join your training and guide!

I send you a big hug!

We keep in touch!

Gabriela Peralta

ALEKS "THE HEBREW HAMMER" SALKIN

"The Result is Confidence in My Body Again"

Hello Aleks,

it's now almost five months since I started working with your material...twice a day the resets and once or twice a day spicing them up with your challenges.The very first thing that occurred has been a strange joy, especially doing baby crawling and rolling. I imagined myself 57 years ago exploring for the first time... and that put that smile on my face...and that joy stayed and makes me ask for more, resulting in exercising right now during our vacation four to five times a day, playing and exploring from your material.... harvesting all the benefits that I read about since I started from so many others, like significantly reducing old joint issues of shoulders, knees, back in just a few days, gaining strenght, muscle(as my wife comments telling me:-)and mobility...to feel that good over such a long period of time(and no end in sight) is remarkable! I tried a few bestselling methods in the past fifteen years and none comes even close to the results I get from doing what I learn from your material. Strange , that movements that working as a craftsman are causing trouble have a healing effect doing the resets. Like crawling and rocking improved my wrists and knees.

Mindblowing the one- legged rocking to the knees, Commando rocking to the shoulders, and the mighty dead bug to lower back and shoulder mobility. Neck nodding helped me to relax areas in my neck and shoulders I couldn't consciously relax before... I could continue speaking of the slight changes in posture that make me walk with more balance, letting me grab things overhead without pain....

THE KICK-ASS INSIDER'S GUIDE TO KETTLEBELL COMPLEXES

The result is confidence in my body again , that I don't even know, that it had been steeling itself away a while ago. That gives me hope for the years to come. Thanks to you and what you put out into the world. Also thanks to strongevity. The question , what is my goal with exercising, what do I intend by working out really cleared my view of what I am doing. I cannot go to bed late and wanting to feel more energetic for example.

By the way , exploring the four straight arm exercises of SASS for just two days(all four each day) gave me a massive pump in my upper arms , shoulders and upper lats that I have to turn when I pass a doorframe :-)

But the most amazing effects your material had on my wife...she wrote you yesterday.... But I tell you, for me it has been close to a miracle, seeing her climbing the stairs without help, or even going onto the floor on her knees for rocking and getting up without help... cause not long ago she could walk just a few steps at home and getting up from a chair was a big thing... we almost lost hope and thought that a wheelchair might be the future....

Aleks, may God bless your life , your family and friends and and all your ways in the world....

Have a very good life and thank you for your good work,

Marcus Tepper
GERMANY

ALEKS "THE HEBREW HAMMER" SALKIN

"I am feeling strong, loose and UNINJURED!!!"

"Looking back at my notebook where I track my training, I started the template on 11-11-18......since then, I have gone from 16kg to 18kg on my "medium" get-ups and from 18kg/20kg half get-ups to 22kg on the "heavy" ones.

Rows have all gone up. Light went from 10kg to 12kg, medium from 12kg to 14kg and heavy from 16kg to 18kg.....and those don't even feel that heavy to be honest....

Heavy goblet squats went from 24kg to 28kg in no time at all.

I have been doing medium-heavy single-arm swings at 22kg and double bell swings with 16kg bells, and snatches on the 3rd training day. Snatches are feeling like tossing around cotton balls with my snatch test bell after completing your snatch program with the 16kg bell....

I am LOVING the results of that!!... As far as my L2 skills, they are all feeling good....so I am feeling comfortable with where those are all at.

Overall, I am feeling strong, loose and UNINJURED!!! What a difference from past certs and events."

Shannon McNutt

DISCLOSURES AND DISCLAIMERS

This publication is published in print format. All trademarks and service marks are the properties of their respective owners. All references to these properties are made solely for editorial purposes. Except for marks actually owned by the Author or the Publisher, no commercial claims are made to their use, and neither the Author nor the Publisher is affiliated with such marks in any way.

Unless otherwise expressly noted, none of the individuals or business entities mentioned herein has endorsed the contents of this publication.

Limits of Liability & Disclaimers of Warranties

Because this publication is a general educational information product, it is not a substitute for professional advice on the topics discussed in it.

The materials in this publication are provided "as is" and without warranties of any kind either express or implied. The Author and the Publisher disclaim all warranties, express or implied, including, but not limited to, implied warranties of merchantability and fitness for a particular purpose. The Author and the Publisher do not warrant that any defects will be corrected. The Author does not warrant or make any representations regarding the use or the results of the use of the materials in this publication in terms of their correctness, accuracy, reliability, or otherwise. Applicable law may not allow the exclusion of implied warranties, so the above exclusion may not apply to you.

Under no circumstances, including, but not limited to, negligence, shall the Author or the Publisher be liable for any special or consequential damages that result from the use of, or the inability to use this publication, even if the Author, the Publisher, or an authorized representative has been advised of the possibility of such damages. Applicable law may not allow the limitation or exclusion of liability or incidental or consequential damages, so the above limitation or exclusion may not apply to you. In no event shall the Author or Publisher total liability to you for all damages, losses, and causes of action (whether in contract, tort, including but not limited to, negligence or otherwise) exceed the amount paid by you, if any, for this publication.

You agree to hold the Author and the Publisher of this publication, principals, agents, affiliates, and employees harmless from any and all liability for all claims for damages due to injuries, including attorney fees and costs, incurred by you or caused to third parties by you, arising out of the products, services, and activities discussed in this publication, excepting only claims for gross negligence or intentional tort.

You agree that any and all claims for gross negligence or intentional tort shall be settled solely by confidential binding arbitration per the American Arbitration Association's commercial arbitration rules. Your claim cannot be aggregated with third party claims. All arbitration must occur in Douglas County, Nebraska where the Author's principal place of business is located. Arbitration fees and costs shall be split equally, and you are solely responsible for your own lawyer fees.

Facts and information are believed to be accurate at the time they were placed in this publication. All data provided in this publication is to be used for information purposes only. The information contained within is not intended to provide specific legal, financial, tax, physical or mental health advice, or any other advice whatsoever, for any individual or company and should not be relied upon in that regard. The services described are only offered in jurisdictions where they may be legally offered. Information provided is not all-inclusive, and is limited to information that is made available and such information should not be relied upon as all-inclusive or accurate.

For more information about this policy, please contact the Author at the e-mail address listed in the Copyright Notice at the front of this publication.

IF YOU DO NOT AGREE WITH THESE TERMS AND EXPRESS CONDITIONS, DO NOT READ THIS PUBLICATION. YOUR USE OF THIS PUBLICATION, INCLUDING PRODUCTS, SERVICES, AND ANY PARTICIPATION IN ACTIVITIES MENTIONED IN THIS PUBLICATION, MEAN THAT YOU ARE AGREEING TO BE LEGALLY BOUND BY THESE TERMS.

Affiliate Compensation & Material Connections Disclosure

This publication may contain references to websites and information created and maintained by other individuals and organizations. The Author and the Publisher do not control or guarantee the accuracy, completeness, relevance, or timeliness of any information or privacy policies posted on these websites.

ALEKS "THE HEBREW HAMMER" SALKIN

You should assume that all references to products and services in this publication are made because material connections exist between the Author or Publisher and the providers of the mentioned products and services ("Provider"). You should also assume that all website links within this publication are affiliate links for (a) the Author, (b) the Publisher, or (c) someone else who is an affiliate for the mentioned products and services (individually and collectively, the "Affiliate").

The Affiliate recommends products and services in this publication based in part on a good faith belief that the purchase of such products or services will help readers in general.

The Affiliate has this good faith belief because (a) the Affiliate has tried the product or service mentioned prior to recommending it or (b) the Affiliate has researched the reputation of the Provider and has made the decision to recommend the Provider's products or services based on the Provider's history of providing these or other products or services.

The representations made by the Affiliate about products and services reflect the Affiliate's honest opinion based upon the facts known to the Affiliate at the time this publication was published.

Because there is a material connection between the Affiliate and Providers of products or services mentioned in this publication, you should always assume that the Affiliate may be biased because of the Affiliate's relationship with a Provider and/or because the Affiliate has received or will receive something of value from a Provider.

Perform your own due diligence before purchasing a product or service mentioned in this publication.

THE KICK-ASS INSIDER'S GUIDE TO KETTLEBELL COMPLEXES

The type of compensation received by the Affiliate may vary. In some instances, the Affiliate may receive complimentary products (such as a review copy), services, or money from a Provider prior to mentioning the Provider's products or services in this publication.

In addition, the Affiliate may receive a monetary commission or non-monetary compensation when you take action by using a website link within this publication. This includes, but is not limited to, when you purchase a product or service from a Provider after going to a website link contained in this publication.

Health Disclaimers

As an express condition to reading this publication, you understand and agree to the following terms.

This publication is a general educational health-related information product. This publication does not contain medical advice.

The publication's content is not a substitute for direct, personal, professional medical care and diagnosis. None of the exercises or treatments (including products and services) mentioned in this publication should be performed or otherwise used without prior approval from your physician or other qualified professional health care provider.

There may be risks associated with participating in activities or using products and services mentioned in this publication for people in poor health or with pre-existing physical or mental health conditions.

Because these risks exist, you will not use such products or participate in such activities if you are in poor health or have a pre-existing mental or physical condition. If you choose to participate in these risks, you do so of your own free will and accord, knowingly and voluntarily assuming all risks associated with such activities.

Purchase Price

Although the Publisher believes the price is fair for the value that you receive, you understand and agree that the purchase price for this publication has been arbitrarily set by the Publisher or the vendor who sold you this publication. This price bears no relationship to objective standards.

Due Diligence

You are advised to do your own due diligence when it comes to making any decisions. Use caution and seek the advice of qualified professionals before acting upon the contents of this publication or any other information. You shall not consider any examples, documents, or other content in this publication or otherwise provided by the Author or Publisher to be the equivalent of professional advice.

The Author and the Publisher assume no responsibility for any losses or damages resulting from your use of any link, information, or opportunity contained in this publication or within any other information disclosed by the Author or the Publisher in any form whatsoever.

YOU SHOULD ALWAYS CONDUCT YOUR OWN INVESTIGATION (PERFORM DUE DILIGENCE) BEFORE BUYING PRODUCTS OR SERVICES FROM ANYONE. THIS INCLUDES PRODUCTS AND SERVICES SOLD VIA WEBSITE LINKS REFERENCED IN THIS PUBLICATION.

Printed in Great Britain
by Amazon